A little book of Prayers for Parents

by Mary Barrett

Dedicated to
my parents Max and Joan Palfrey,
who truly are parents of prayer

First published 2004
Copyright © 2004
Reprinted 2005

All rights reserved. No part of this publication
may be reproduced in any form without prior
permission from the publisher.

British Library Cataloguing in Publication Data.
A catalogue record for this book is available
from the British Library.

ISBN 1-903921-15-5

Published by
Autumn House
Grantham, Lincs.
Printed in Thailand.

INTRODUCTION

We long for the best for our children but, as parents, are limited in what we can do. That is not the case with God; he is able to bless our children with every good thing.

This little book is to help us as parents to pray for our children. The Bible texts cover the sorts of things that we all long for our children to experience – including a relationship with God.

Carry the book with you wherever you are. When you are able to do so, flick through it and find the appropriate Bible promise and prayer for your child. The prayers are short, so you can pray anywhere!

One of the greatest things we can do for our children is to pray for them. We are never limited in giving our children the best when we pray and ask God to do what we are unable to do. So go on – pray for your children, stand back, and let God work in their lives!

All texts are taken from the New International Version
(Hodder and Stoughton, 1998).

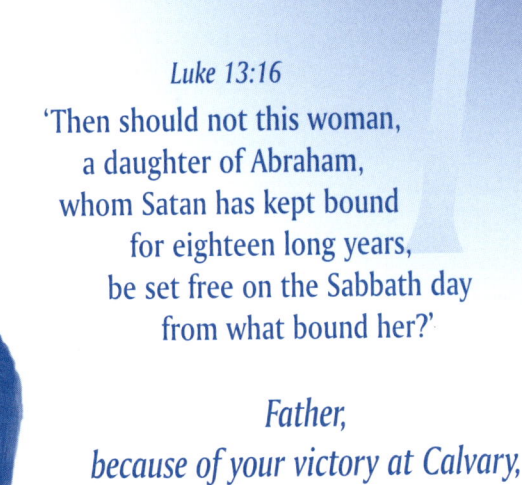

Luke 13:16
'Then should not this woman,
a daughter of Abraham,
whom Satan has kept bound
for eighteen long years,
be set free on the Sabbath day
from what bound her?'

*Father,
because of your victory at Calvary,
set my children free from those
things that Satan is using to bind
them to him.*

Psalm 19:10

'They are more precious than gold,
than much pure gold;
they are sweeter than honey,
than honey from the comb.'

*Father God,
help my children to realise that
true wealth is taking delight
in your Word.*

Ephesians 2:10

'For we are God's workmanship,
created in Christ Jesus to do good works,
which God prepared in advance for us to do.'

*Father in Heaven,
thank you that you created us to
do good. Please help my children
to find satisfaction in being
gracious to others.*

Psalm 51:10
'Create in me a pure heart, O God,
and renew a steadfast spirit with me.'

Holy Father,
nurture within my children a desire
for what is pure and grant them
the determination to pursue it.

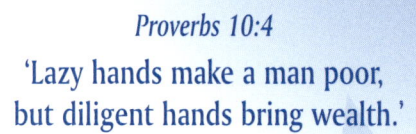

Proverbs 10:4
'Lazy hands make a man poor,
but diligent hands bring wealth.'

*Dear Father,
may laziness never be prominent
in my children's lives. Help them
to be dedicated workers who
will see success in their work.*

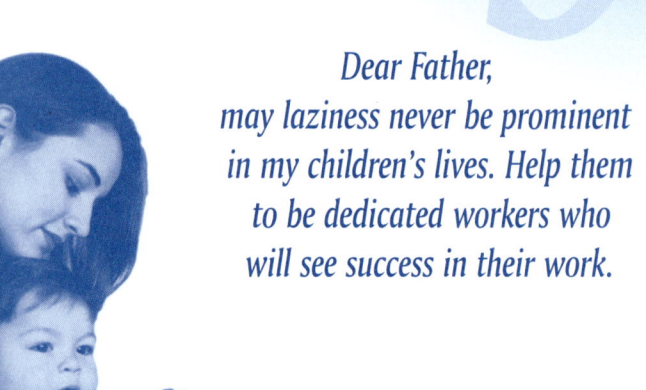

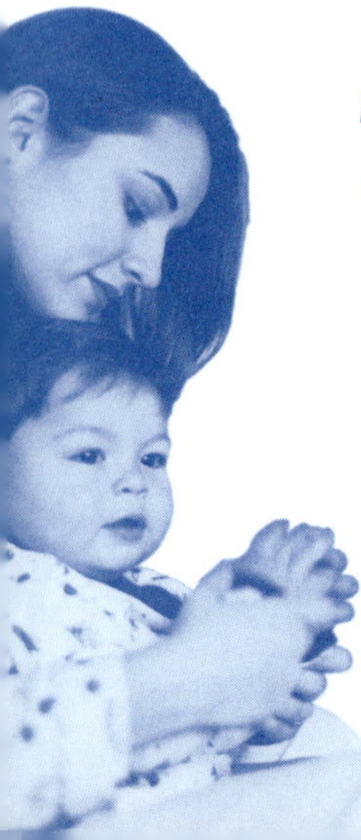

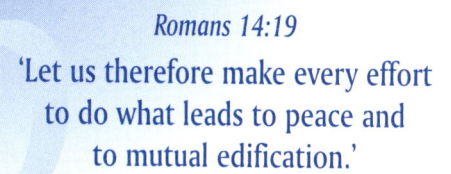

Romans 14:19
'Let us therefore make every effort
to do what leads to peace and
to mutual edification.'

*Father God,
grant my children the desire
to bring peace and harmony
into any situation where
conflict may arise.*

7

Isaiah 43:18, 19
'Forget the former things; do not dwell on the past.
See, I am doing a new thing.'

Dear Father,
help my children not to focus continually on the past or be consumed with regret. Develop within them an attitude that is forward looking, based on your ability to do 'a new thing'.

Philippians 4:13
'I can do everything
through him who gives me strength.'

*Father God,
help my children to learn to
depend on your strength.*

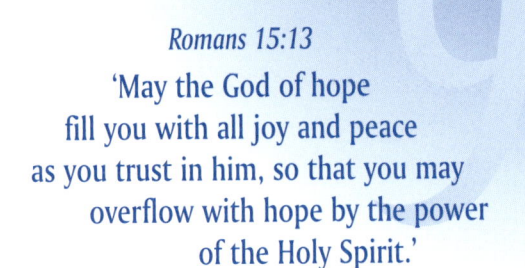

Romans 15:13
'May the God of hope
fill you with all joy and peace
as you trust in him, so that you may
overflow with hope by the power
of the Holy Spirit.'

I ask, Father,
that my children may grow to be
confident, optimistic and positive.

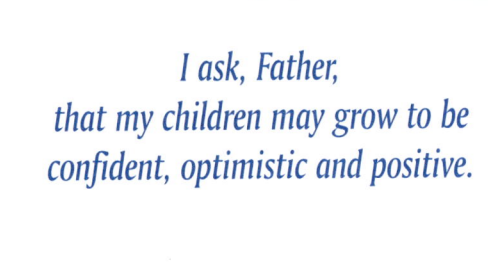

10

Ephesians 6:18

'And pray in the Spirit on all occasions with all kinds of prayers and requests. With this in mind, be alert, and always keep on praying for all the saints.'

Whatever situations occur in my children's lives, may they, and I, turn to you first for the solution.

11

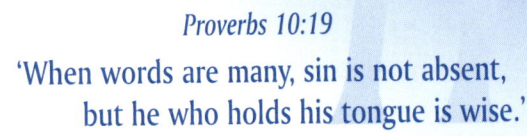

Proverbs 10:19
'When words are many, sin is not absent,
but he who holds his tongue is wise.'

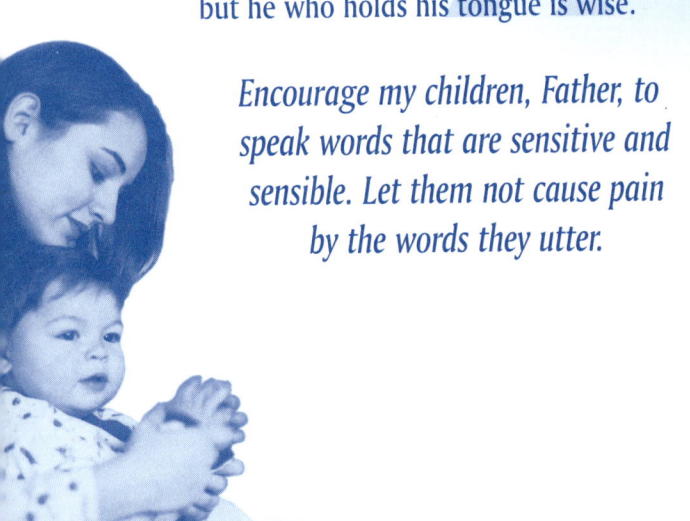

Encourage my children, Father, to speak words that are sensitive and sensible. Let them not cause pain by the words they utter.

Matthew 10:42

'And if anyone gives even a cup of cold water to one of these little ones because he is my disciple, I tell you the truth, he will certainly not lose his reward.'

*Abba Father,
place within my children's hearts
your love, so that they may seek to
relieve the pain of those who suffer.*

Isaiah 43:2

'When you pass through the waters,
I will be with you;
and when you pass through the rivers,
they will not sweep over you.
When you walk through the fire
you will not be burned;
the flames will not set you ablaze.'

*Father of Comfort,
whatever situations my children
may go through, may they always
sense your presence, your love
and your power.*

14

Isaiah 54:13
'All your sons will be taught by the Lord, and great will be your children's peace.'

*Father,
please keep your promise.
Be a teacher to my children and grant them as much peace as possible, in their hearts and in their lives.*

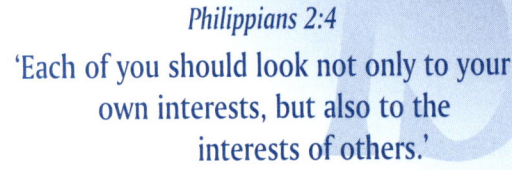

Philippians 2:4
'Each of you should look not only to your own interests, but also to the interests of others.'

*God in Heaven,
may selfishness never take hold of my children's lives. Teach them to care for others just as much as they care for themselves.*

16

Matthew 7:1-3

'Do not judge, or you too will be judged. . . .
Why do you look at the speck of sawdust
in your brother's eye and pay no attention
to the plank in your own eye?'

*Dear Father,
help my children not to be eager
to look for the faults in others;
but rather to be aware of
their own weaknesses.*

Jeremiah 29:11
' "For I know the plans I have for you,"
declares the Lord, "plans to prosper
you and not to harm you, plans to
give you hope and a future." '

*Father God,
may my children never live
with a spirit of hopelessness.
Let them know that you always
have the best in mind for them.*

Romans 5:8
'But God demonstrates his own love for us in this:
While we were still sinners,
Christ died for us.'

Father God
help my children to know in their
hearts and minds the depth of
love that you have for them, even
though sin may cause them to
think otherwise.

Hebrews 12:14
'Make every effort to live in peace with all men
and to be holy; without holiness no-one
will see the Lord.'

*Father,
let your peace and your holiness
guide the way my children live.*

John 1:45
'Philip found Nathanael and told him,
"We have found the one Moses wrote about in the
Law, and about whom the prophets also wrote –
Jesus of Nazareth, the son of Joseph." '

*Father,
may my children have a desire
to share with others their
relationship with you. Give them
many opportunities to say, 'I have
found Jesus, the Son of God.'*

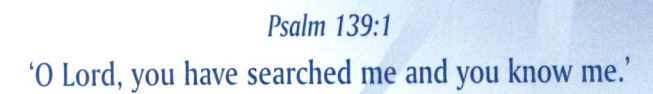

Psalm 139:1
'O Lord, you have searched me and you know me.'

Loving Father,
may my children know that they do
not need to hide anything from you,
for you will always love and
accept them.

22

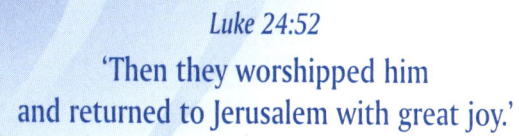

Luke 24:52
'Then they worshipped him
and returned to Jerusalem with great joy.'

*Almighty Father God,
teach my children how to worship you.
As a result, may they experience
real joy in their hearts.*

1 John 1:9

'If we confess our sins,
he is faithful and just and will forgive us our sins
and purify us from all unrighteousness.'

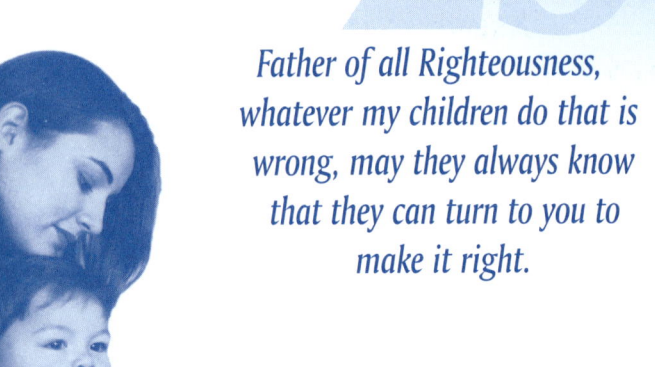

*Father of all Righteousness,
whatever my children do that is
wrong, may they always know
that they can turn to you to
make it right.*

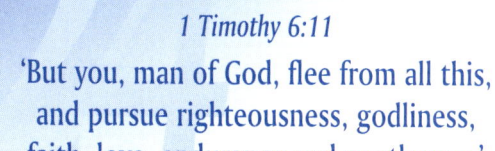

1 Timothy 6:11
'But you, man of God, flee from all this,
and pursue righteousness, godliness,
faith, love, endurance and gentleness.'

*Father,
may my children truly become
your children and may your values
become their values.*

Romans 12:16

'Live in harmony with one another.
Do not be proud, but be willing to associate
with people of low position.'

*Father,
give my children the gift of being
able to associate with anyone.
Help them to be humble and
yet confident.*

Isaiah 48:17
'"I am the Lord your God,
who teaches you what is best for you,
who directs you in the way you should go."'

*Father,
there will be many times when my
children will be unsure of the right
decisions to make. Please direct
them in such a way that the very
best will always happen for them.*

Romans 12:15
'Rejoice with those who rejoice;
mourn with those who mourn.'

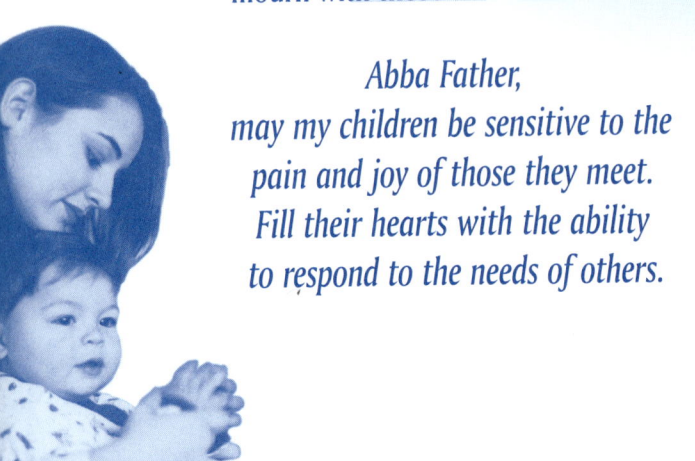

*Abba Father,
may my children be sensitive to the
pain and joy of those they meet.
Fill their hearts with the ability
to respond to the needs of others.*

1 Thessalonians 4:11, 12
'Make it your ambition to lead a quiet life, . . .
so that your daily life may win the respect of
outsiders and so that you will not be
dependent on anybody.'

*Father God,
may the strongest ambition of my
children be to live in such a way
that they will help others to see you.*

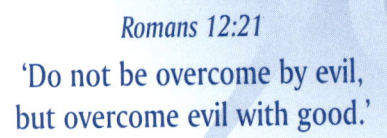

Romans 12:21
'Do not be overcome by evil,
but overcome evil with good.'

*Father of Goodness,
may retaliation and revenge never
be resident in my children's hearts
when they are hurt by evil. Instead,
Father, fill their hearts with your
love, so that they can respond
with loving actions and
forgiving thoughts.*

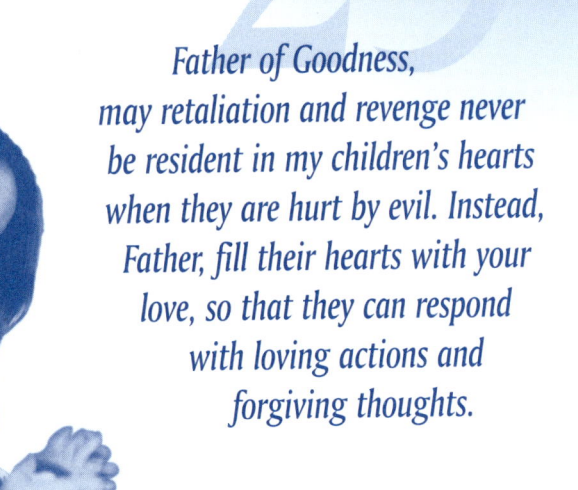

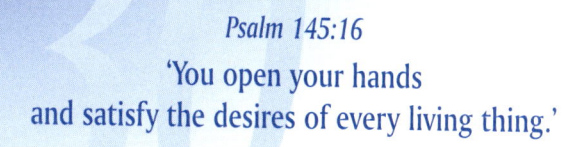

Psalm 145:16
'You open your hands
and satisfy the desires of every living thing.'

*Father,
open your hand to my children and
fill their hearts with your blessings.*

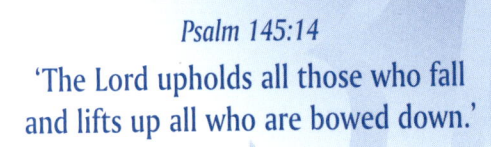

Psalm 145:14
'The Lord upholds all those who fall
and lifts up all who are bowed down.'

*Father of Compassion,
when my children fall down because
of the pressures of life, may you be
the One to lift them up.*

32

Psalm 37:4
'Delight yourself in the Lord and he will give you the desires of your heart.'

*Father,
may my children find fulfilment in their relationship with you, and may the dreams tucked away in their hearts that arise from that relationship be realised.*

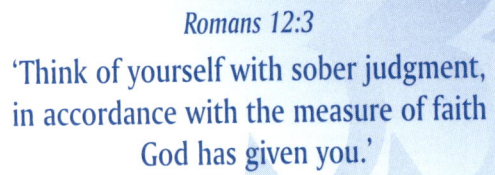

Romans 12:3
'Think of yourself with sober judgment,
in accordance with the measure of faith
God has given you.'

*Father,
give my children a mighty measure
of faith, so that they will never
be overwhelmed by doubt.*

Luke 2:52
'And Jesus grew in wisdom and stature,
and in favour with God and men.'

*Quite simply, Father God,
help my children to grow
as Jesus did when he was on earth.*

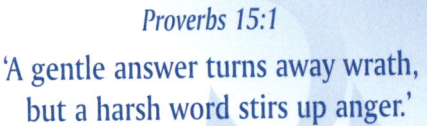

Proverbs 15:1
'A gentle answer turns away wrath,
but a harsh word stirs up anger.'

*Father of Peace,
teach my children to respond to
conflict with a gentle answer
instead of an angry word.*

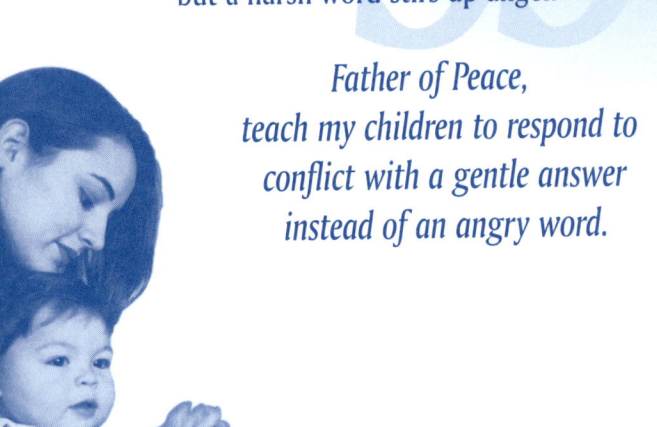

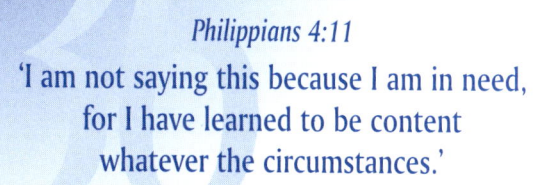

Philippians 4:11
'I am not saying this because I am in need,
for I have learned to be content
whatever the circumstances.'

*Father
when life fails to meet my children's
expectations, may their friendship
with you be strong enough
to carry them through.*

Deuteronomy 8:3
'He humbled you, causing you to hunger
and then feeding you with manna, which neither
you nor your fathers had known, to teach you
that man does not live on bread alone
but on every word that comes from
the mouth of the Lord.'

*Dear Father,
I give you permission to do what
you need to do, so that my children
will seek you more than anything
this world offers. Cause them to
hunger for you and then feed
them as only you can.*

38

Psalm 27:14
'Wait for the Lord,
be strong and take heart
and wait for the Lord.'

*Father God,
it is never easy to be patient,
but teach my children that by
waiting upon you, they can save
themselves the pain of wrong
decisions and wrong choices.*

Proverbs 8:17, 18
'I love those who love me, and those who seek me find me. With me are riches and honour, enduring wealth and prosperity.'

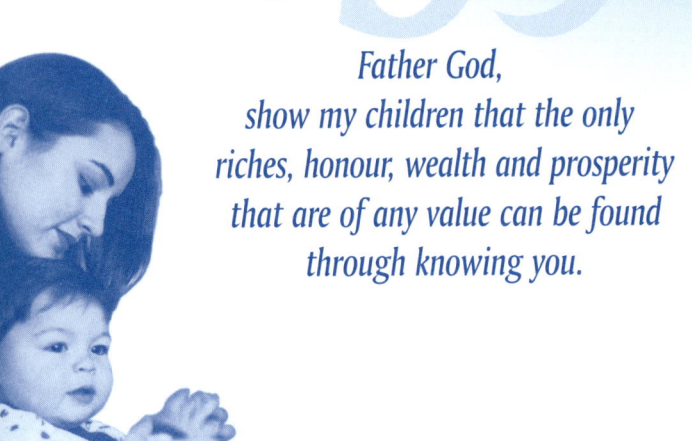

*Father God,
show my children that the only riches, honour, wealth and prosperity that are of any value can be found through knowing you.*

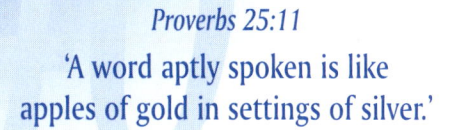

Proverbs 25:11
'A word aptly spoken is like
apples of gold in settings of silver.'

*Father God,
teach my children to speak words
that are appealing and attractive,
and not critical and condemning.*

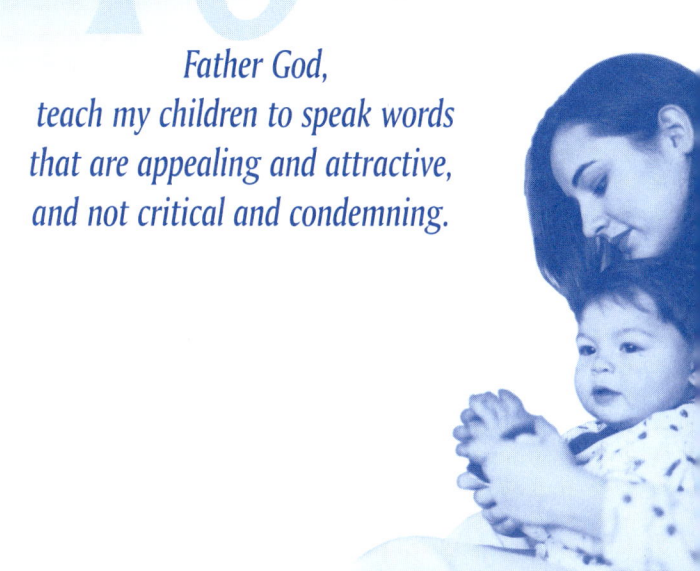

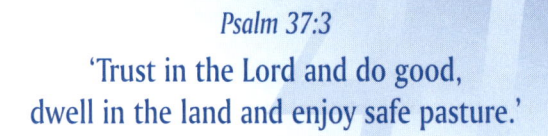

Psalm 37:3
'Trust in the Lord and do good,
dwell in the land and enjoy safe pasture.'

*Father God,
deepen the desire within my
children's hearts to depend upon you.
Encourage them to do good to
others. May they then live
secure in you.*

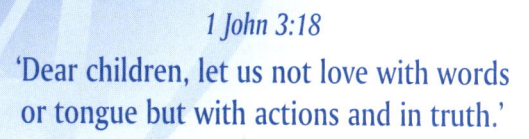

1 John 3:18
'Dear children, let us not love with words
or tongue but with actions and in truth.'

*Abba Father,
may others be confident that my
children will do what they
say they will.*

Ecclesiastes 3:22
'So I saw that there is nothing better for a man than to enjoy his work, because that is his lot.'

*Father,
lead my children to the life-work
that will give them satisfaction
and joy.*

Proverbs 22:6
'Train a child in the way he should go,
and when he is old he will not turn from it.'

Father,
help me to bring up my children
in such a way that their natural
instinct will be to follow you.

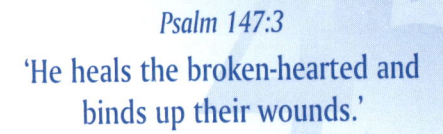

Psalm 147:3
'He heals the broken-hearted and
binds up their wounds.'

Father,
whatever pains and hurts my
children go through may they
always know that you will bring
healing and hope.

Proverbs 28:14
'Blessed is the man who always fears the Lord,
but he who hardens his heart falls into trouble.'

*Father,
may my children have a respect for
you that will never be broken and
may their hearts always be open
to your voice, your influence, and
your guidance.*

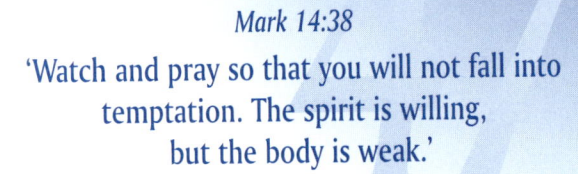

Mark 14:38
'Watch and pray so that you will not fall into temptation. The spirit is willing, but the body is weak.'

*Father of Power,
help my children to say 'No'
when temptations come their way.*

Galatians 5:22, 23
'But the fruit of the Spirit is love, joy, peace, patience, kindness, goodness, faithfulness, gentleness and self-control.'

*Gentle Father,
may the fruit of your Spirit
grow in abundance in the lives
of my children, so that others
recognise you in them.*

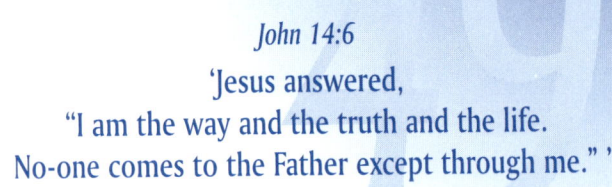

John 14:6
'Jesus answered,
"I am the way and the truth and the life.
No-one comes to the Father except through me." '

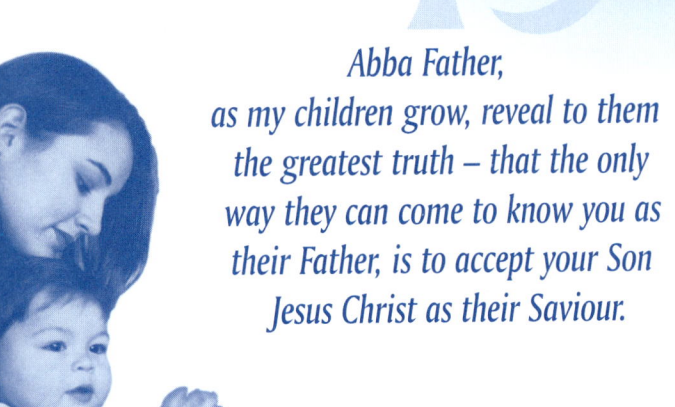

*Abba Father,
as my children grow, reveal to them
the greatest truth – that the only
way they can come to know you as
their Father, is to accept your Son
Jesus Christ as their Saviour.*

Hebrews 12:15
'See to it that no-one misses the grace of God
and that no bitter root grows up
to cause trouble and defile many.'

*Father God,
if there be any bitterness within my
children please pull it out so that
your grace may grow there instead.*

Matthew 19:26

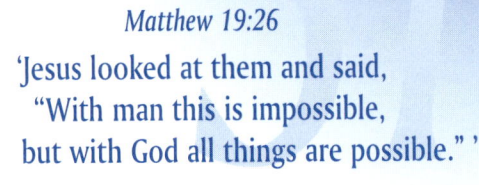

'Jesus looked at them and said,
"With man this is impossible,
but with God all things are possible." '

*Father of Possibilities,
may my children know that any
roadblocks they encounter in
their lives can be pushed aside
by your power.*

Matthew 25:15
'To one he gave five talents of money,
to another two talents, and to another one talent,
each according to his ability.
Then he went on his journey.'

*Father in Heaven,
help my children to be content
with the ability you have given them.
Help them to fulfil their potential,
appreciate the gifts of others, and
not feel threatened by them.*

Philippians 4:8

'Finally brothers, whatever is true, whatever is noble, whatever is right, whatever is pure, whatever is lovely, whatever is admirable – if anything is excellent or praiseworthy – think about such things.'

*Father of Righteousness,
help my children to be conscious of
what they see, hear, think and do.
May their choices reflect their
relationship with you.*

Psalm 73:26
'My flesh and my heart may fail,
but God is the strength of my heart
and my portion forever.'

*Father,
when my children are full of
fear, enable them to focus on your
faithfulness and fill their hearts
with your fearlessness.*

Hebrews 13:5
'Keep your lives free from the love of money
and be content with what you have, because
God has said, "Never will I leave you;
never will I forsake you."'

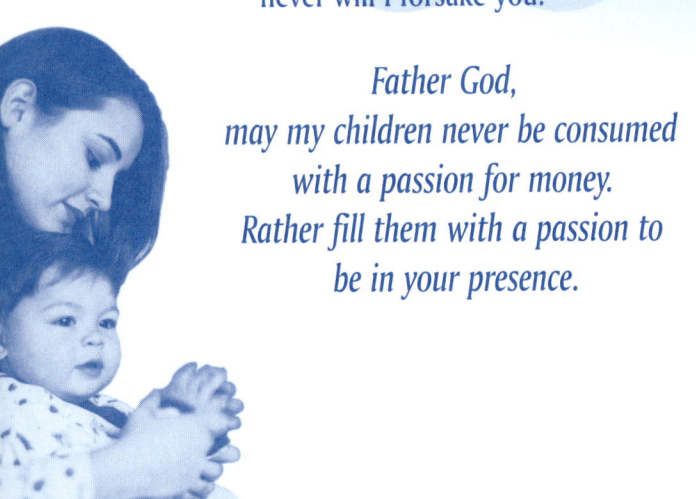

*Father God,
may my children never be consumed
with a passion for money.
Rather fill them with a passion to
be in your presence.*

Romans 8:28

'And we know that in all things
God works for the good of those who love him,
who have been called according
to his purpose.'

*Father,
whatever is going on in my
children's lives, may they always
know that you can bring
something good out of it.*

Psalm 144:15
'Blessed are the people of whom this is true;
blessed are the people whose God is the Lord.'

Father of Grace,
May your blessings rest upon my
children today. And may you be the
Lord of their lives.

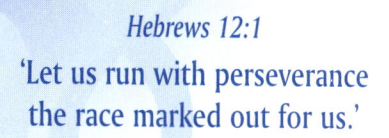

Hebrews 12:1
'Let us run with perseverance
the race marked out for us.'

*Father God,
help my children not to give up when
things get tough, but give them the
ability to keep on going.*

Matthew 6:24

'No-one can serve two masters.
Either he will hate the one and love the other, or he will be devoted to the one and despise the other.
You cannot serve both God and Money.'

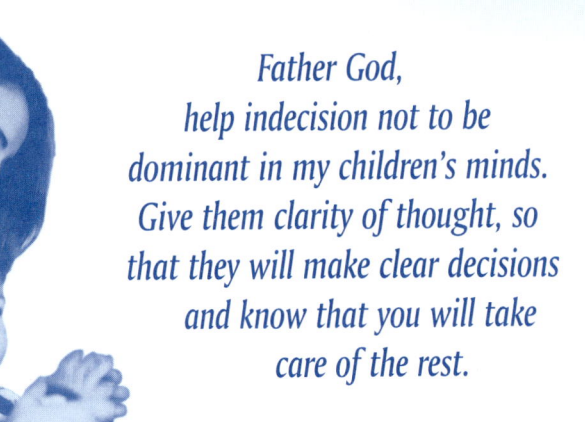

*Father God,
help indecision not to be dominant in my children's minds. Give them clarity of thought, so that they will make clear decisions and know that you will take care of the rest.*

Ephesians 4:31
'Get rid of all bitterness,
rage and anger, brawling and slander,
along with every form of malice.'

*Father of love,
may godless characteristics be
absent from my children's lives.
May their hearts overflow with
your loving kindness instead of
the ugliness of sin.*

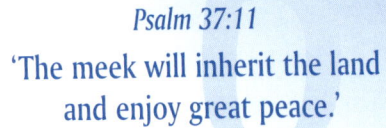

Psalm 37:11
'The meek will inherit the land
and enjoy great peace.'

*Gentle Father,
I ask that my children will wear your mantle of meekness, rather than a coat of pride. May you also clothe them with your peace.*

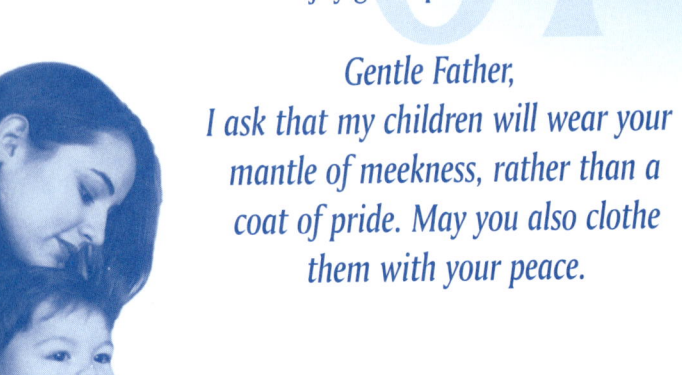

Daniel 1:15
'At the end of the ten days they looked healthier and better nourished than any of the young men who ate the royal food.'

*Father,
please place within my children the desire to eat what is good rather than what is bad. Give them an appetite for the food that will make them healthy and strong.*

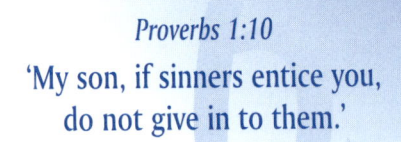

Proverbs 1:10
'My son, if sinners entice you,
do not give in to them.'

*Father of Strength,
help my children to be strong
enough to stand up to those who
will tempt them to do that which
they shouldn't.*

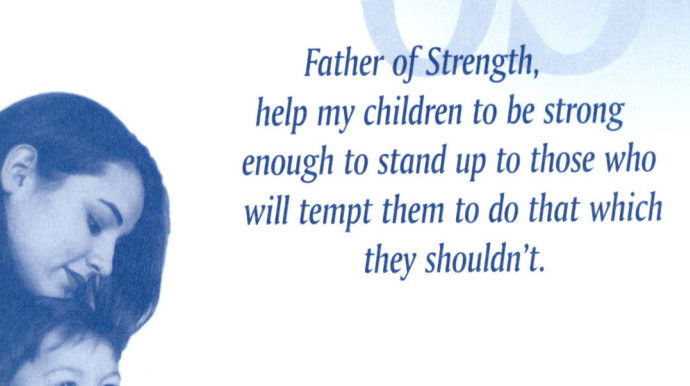

Ecclesiastes 7:21
'Do not pay attention to every word people say,
or you may hear your servant cursing you.'

Help my children not to be concerned about what others think of them, rather to focus on your acceptance of them. When they are criticised may they discard what is not true and give it no further thought.

2 Chronicles 31:21

'In everything that he undertook in the service of God's temple and in obedience to the law and the commands, he sought his God and worked wholeheartedly. And so he prospered.'

*Father,
in whatever work my children do,
let them do it with enthusiasm and
energy. May they experience success
in every aspect of their work.*

1 Samuel 16:7
'But the Lord said to Samuel, "Do not consider his appearance or his height, for I have rejected him. The Lord does not look at the things people look at. Man looks at the outward appearance, but the Lord looks at the heart." '

*Father,
teach my children not to dismiss
those who do not look the way
society says they should look.
Teach my children to be like you
and to look at a person's heart.*

Matthew 4:4
'Jesus answered, "It is written:
'Man does not live on bread alone, but on every word that comes from the mouth of God.'"'

*Father,
may my children hunger after you,
more than hungering for the bread
of this world.*

Numbers 6:24-26

'The Lord bless you and keep you,
the Lord make his face shine upon you and be
gracious to you; the Lord turn his face towards
you and give you peace.'

*Gracious Father,
may my children experience
what it is to be blessed by you,
to be warmed by the sunshine of
your love, to look in your direction
and to receive your gift of peace.*

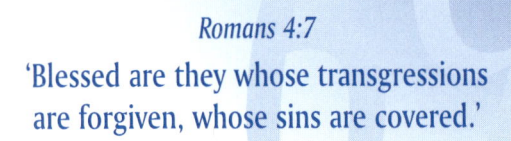

Romans 4:7
'Blessed are they whose transgressions
are forgiven, whose sins are covered.'

*Forgiving Father,
help my children to have the
assurance that their sins will never
be uncovered when they have
been forgiven by you.*

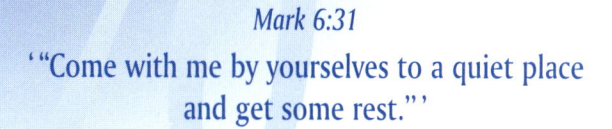

Mark 6:31
' "Come with me by yourselves to a quiet place
and get some rest." '

*Father of Rest,
when life gets difficult,
lead my children to you so
that they can be refreshed and
replenished by your Spirit of calm.*

Isaiah 49:25
'But this is what the Lord says:
. . . "I will contend with those
who contend with you,
and your children I will save."'

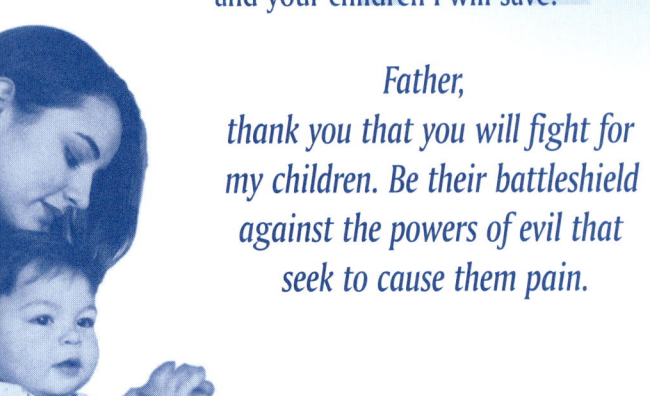

*Father,
thank you that you will fight for
my children. Be their battleshield
against the powers of evil that
seek to cause them pain.*

3 John 4
'I have no greater joy than to hear that my children are walking in the truth.'

*Father,
teach my children to place their
footsteps in yours and to walk
in the way of righteousness.*

Matthew 18:14

' "In the same way your Father in heaven is not willing that any of these little ones should be lost." '

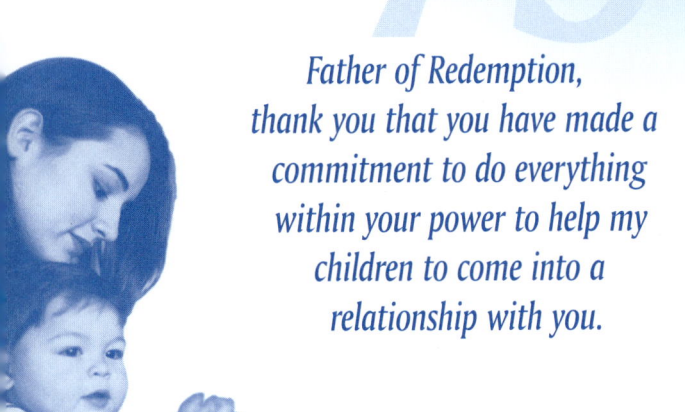

*Father of Redemption,
thank you that you have made a
commitment to do everything
within your power to help my
children to come into a
relationship with you.*

Acts 2:38

'"Repent and be baptised, every one of you, in the name of Jesus Christ for the forgiveness of your sins. And you will receive the gift of the Holy Spirit."'

*Father,
may you whisper those words to my
children's hearts. Let them know
of your love, your forgiveness and
your gift of the Holy Spirit.*

Daniel 1:17

'To these four young men God gave knowledge and understanding of all kinds of literature and learning.'

*Father,
where my children struggle academically, may you supply what they need, so that they can succeed in the way that you want them to.*

Romans 10:17

'Consequently, faith comes from hearing the message, and the message is heard through the word of Christ.'

*Father of Faith,
encourage my children to read your word. May they understand and take delight in what they read, and may it deepen their confidence in you.*

Galatians 4:19

'My dear children, for whom I am again in the pains of childbirth until Christ is formed in you.'

Father,
May you patiently and lovingly work with my children. Help them to have the character of Jesus imprinted upon their hearts.

Jeremiah 31:3
'"I have loved you with an everlasting love;
I have drawn you with loving-kindness."'

*Father,
you love like no other.
Speak to my children so
that they may realise that.*

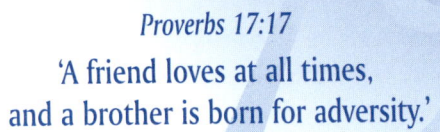

Proverbs 17:17
'A friend loves at all times,
and a brother is born for adversity.'

*Father,
teach my children to be dedicated,
dependable and devoted to their
family and friends.*

Psalm 5:3
'In the morning, O Lord, you hear my voice;
in the morning I lay my requests before you
and wait in expectation.'

*Father of the Sunrise,
help my children to know that
as they awake you are with them,
eager to hear what is on their hearts.*

Matthew 7:12
'So in everything, do to others what you would have them do to you.'

Father,
may your rule of life
be my children's rule of life.

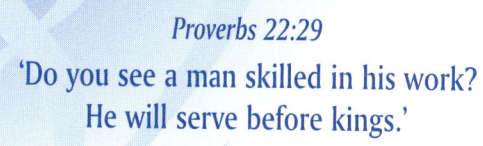

Proverbs 22:29
'Do you see a man skilled in his work?
He will serve before kings.'

*Father,
help my children to develop the skills
that you have given them. Help
them to settle in their workplace
and serve with excellence.*

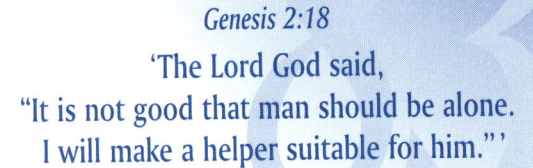

Genesis 2:18
'The Lord God said,
"It is not good that man should be alone.
I will make a helper suitable for him."'

*Father God,
you know how we need that special
someone to love and to love us.
Please lead my daughter/son to the
marriage partner who will truly be
a soul-mate to her/him.*

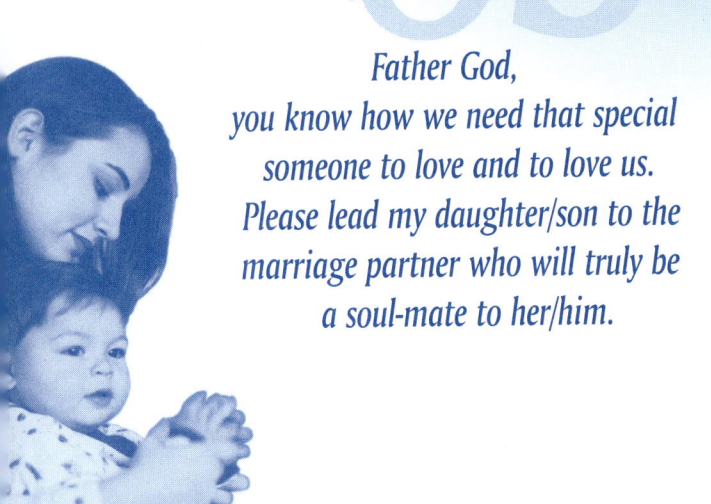

Luke 12:29

'"And do not set your heart on what you will eat or drink; do not worry about it."'

*Dear Father,
help my children never to be overwhelmed by worry. Teach them through experience that they can depend on you to find the perfect solution for their every concern.*

Proverbs 4:7
'Wisdom is supreme; therefore get wisdom.
Though it cost all you have, get understanding.'

*Father God,
bestow upon my children your gift of wisdom – to make the right choices, to choose the right relationships, to manage their finances and to live right.*

Psalm 34:4
'I sought the Lord, and he answered me;
he delivered me from all my fears.'

*Father,
whatever lodges in the minds and
hearts of my children may you
set them free from fear.*

Psalm 130:4
'With you there is forgiveness.'

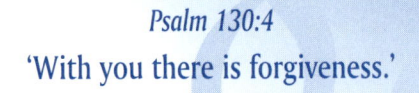

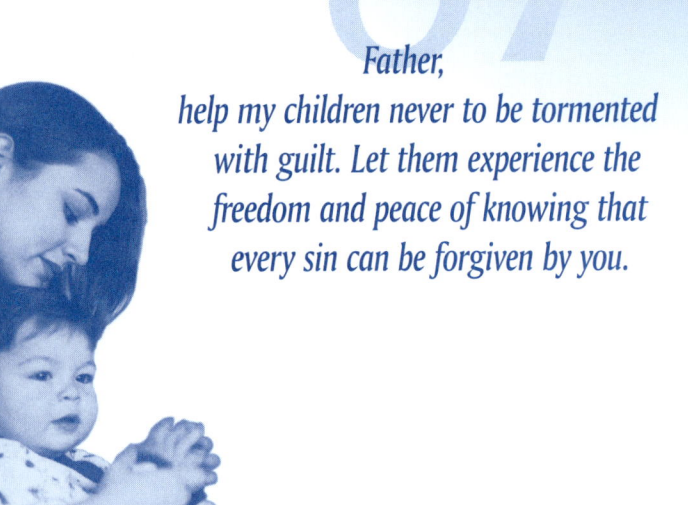

Father,
help my children never to be tormented with guilt. Let them experience the freedom and peace of knowing that every sin can be forgiven by you.

Proverbs 18:24
'A man of many companions may come to ruin, but there is a friend who sticks closer than a brother.'

*Father,
may my children learn that though
they seek many friends, only you
offer them a friendship that
no one can break.*

Psalm 121:7

'The Lord will keep you from all harm –
he will watch over your life; the Lord will watch
over your coming and going both now
and for evermore.'

*Powerful Father,
please protect my children
as they come and go.*

Psalm 32:8
'I will instruct you and teach you
in the way you should go;
I will counsel you and watch over you.'

*Father,
I claim this promise for my children.
Show them clearly which road to
take. May my children be able to
hear your voice when they are
unsure about their future.*

Proverbs 16:7

'When a man's ways are pleasing to the Lord,
he makes even his enemies live at peace with him.'

Father,
teach my children to live in ways that
make you proud of them and hold
back the taunts of those who seek
to make life uncomfortable for them.

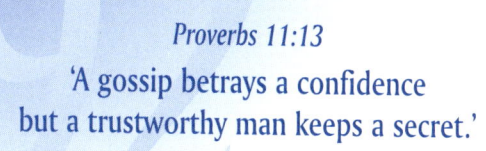

Proverbs 11:13
'A gossip betrays a confidence
but a trustworthy man keeps a secret.'

Father,
help my children not to gossip or
promote it in any way, so that
others might know that my children
can be trusted to keep confidences.

2 Corinthians 12:7

'To keep me from becoming conceited because of these surpassingly great revelations, there was given me a thorn in my flesh.'

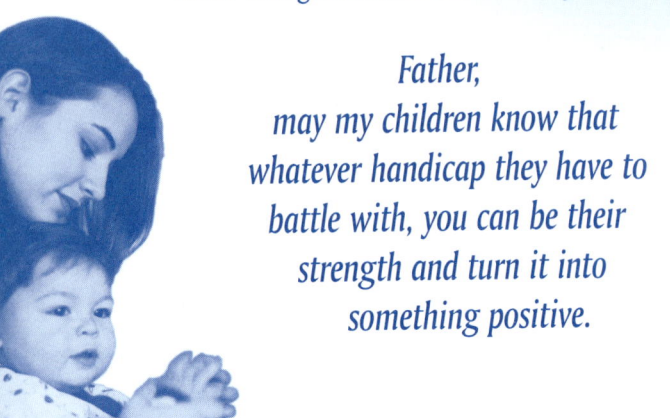

*Father,
may my children know that whatever handicap they have to battle with, you can be their strength and turn it into something positive.*

Proverbs 1:8, 9
'Listen, my son, to your father's instructions
and do not forsake your mother's teaching.
They will be a garland to grace your head
and a chain to adorn your neck.'

*Heavenly Father,
may my children treasure the
counsel that we give them as
they would value precious jewels.*

Exodus 23:25
'"I will take away sickness from among you."'

*Father,
please keep my children healthy,
strong in their bodies, and in their
minds. Instil within them the desire
to do what they can to be healthy.*

Proverbs 4:18
'The path of righteousness is like the first gleam of dawn, shining ever brighter till the full light of day.'

Father,
may my children's relationship with you be such that your influence in their lives will grow stronger and clearer as they mature.

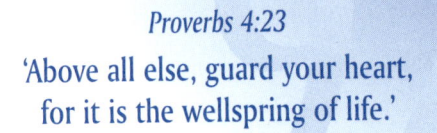

Proverbs 4:23
'Above all else, guard your heart,
for it is the wellspring of life.'

*Dear Father,
stand guard with my children
at the entrance to their hearts.
Encourage them only to allow
that which brings life to have
a place there.*

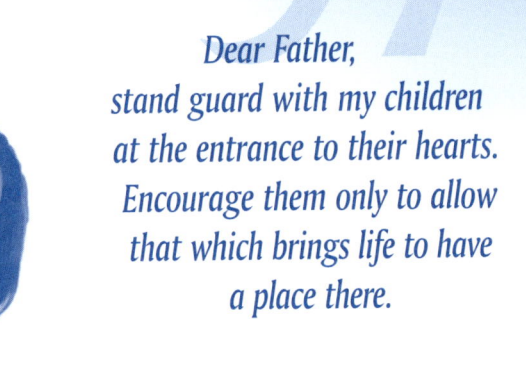

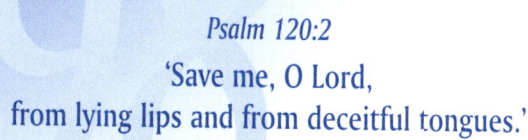

Psalm 120:2
'Save me, O Lord,
from lying lips and from deceitful tongues.'

*God of Power,
help my children not to speak lies or
to deceive others. May honesty and
uprightness be the central core of
their characters.*

Micah 6:8

'He has showed you, O man, what is good.
And what does the Lord require of you?
To act justly and to love mercy and
to walk humbly with your God.'

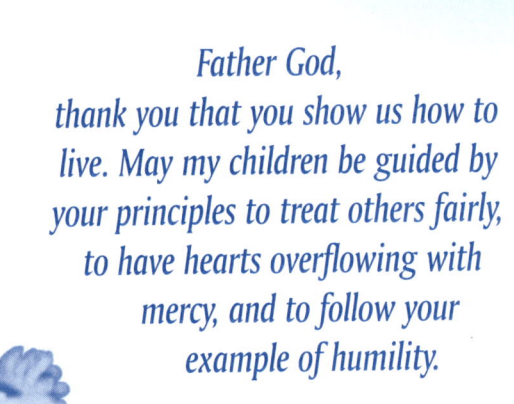

*Father God,
thank you that you show us how to
live. May my children be guided by
your principles to treat others fairly,
to have hearts overflowing with
mercy, and to follow your
example of humility.*

Proverbs 24:27
'Finish your outdoor work
and get your fields ready;
after that, build your house.'

*Father,
help my children to be able to
complete one job before starting
another. Help them not to give
up when things get difficult, but
persevere to finish what they
have started.*

Ephesians 4:32
'Be kind and compassionate to one another,
forgiving each other, just as in Christ
God forgave you.'

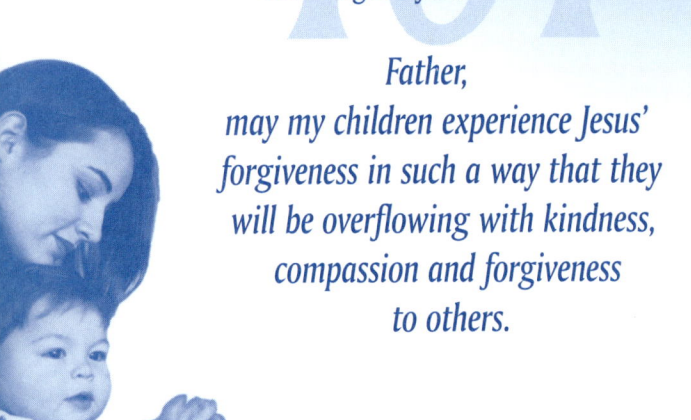

*Father,
may my children experience Jesus'
forgiveness in such a way that they
will be overflowing with kindness,
compassion and forgiveness
to others.*

Deuteronomy 30:19
'I have set before you life and death,
blessings and curses. Now choose life,
so that you and your children may live.'

*Father,
help my children to make good
choices concerning what they take
into their bodies. Help them to
choose to say 'No' to drinks and
drugs and anything that is
harmful to them.*

Joshua 1:8
'Do not let this Book of Law depart from your mouth; meditate on it day and night, so that you may be careful to do everything written in it. Then you will be prosperous and successful.'

*Father,
may my children reach for your Bible when they awake and may they reach for it at night before they go to sleep.*

Daniel 6:10
'Now when Daniel learned that the decree had been published, he went home to his upstairs room where the window opened towards Jerusalem. Three times a day he got down on his knees and prayed, giving thanks to his God, just as he had done before.'

*Father of Mighty Miracles,
help my children to share the same
resolve as Daniel, to pray to you
regularly and never to deny you
even though there may be times
when denial may be the
easiest option.*

105

Romans 15:7
'Accept one another, then, just as Christ accepted you, in order to bring praise to God.'

*Father,
influence my children, by the way you accept all, to respond to others with affection, approval and affirmation.*

Psalm 57:2
'I cry out to God Most High, to God, who fulfils [this purpose] for me.'

*Father,
I've told my children that you have given them special gifts so that they may fulfil a special purpose in life that no one else can. Help them to listen for your voice, so that they may follow your plan for their lives.*

Psalm 91:9, 10
'If you make the Most High your dwelling –
even the Lord, who is my refuge –
then no harm will befall you,
no disaster will come near your tent.'

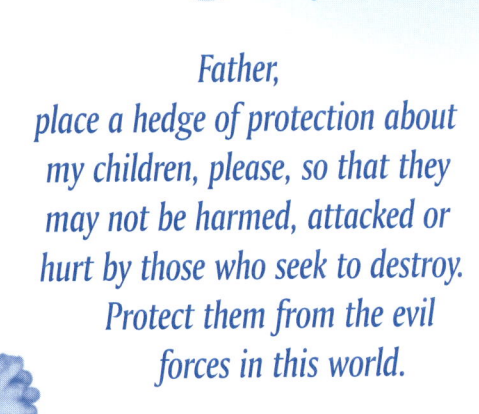

*Father,
place a hedge of protection about
my children, please, so that they
may not be harmed, attacked or
hurt by those who seek to destroy.
Protect them from the evil
forces in this world.*

Psalm 34:10
'Those who seek the Lord
lack no good thing.'

*Generous Father,
thank you for your promise that
when my children pursue a
relationship with you they will
experience your goodness in
their lives. Pour out that
goodness, Father,
in abundance.*

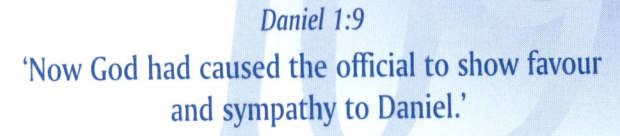

Daniel 1:9
'Now God had caused the official to show favour and sympathy to Daniel.'

*Father,
there will be times when some will not look upon my children positively. Help them to respond to my children favourably.*

110

1 Samuel 3:10

'The Lord came and stood there, calling as at the other times, "Samuel! Samuel!" Then Samuel said, "Speak, for your servant is listening." '

Father,
when my children hear your voice
may they be as eager as Samuel
was to listen to what you
have to say.

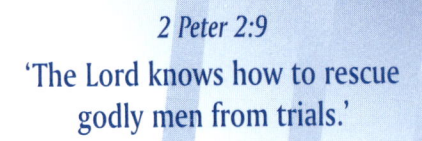

2 Peter 2:9
'The Lord knows how to rescue godly men from trials.'

*Father,
when temptations come to my children, do as you promise; secure their freedom from those things which Satan may use to entice them.*

112

Psalm 37:39
'The Lord . . . is their stronghold
in time of trouble.'

*Father,
be my children's strength
in the tough times of life.*

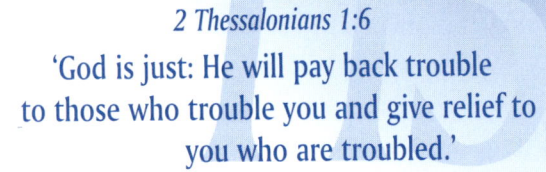

2 Thessalonians 1:6
'God is just: He will pay back trouble to those who trouble you and give relief to you who are troubled.'

*Father,
I don't want my children to take revenge on those who hurt them. May they know that they can trust you to sort things out. Please heal the hurt in my children's hearts as you work to bring about justice.*

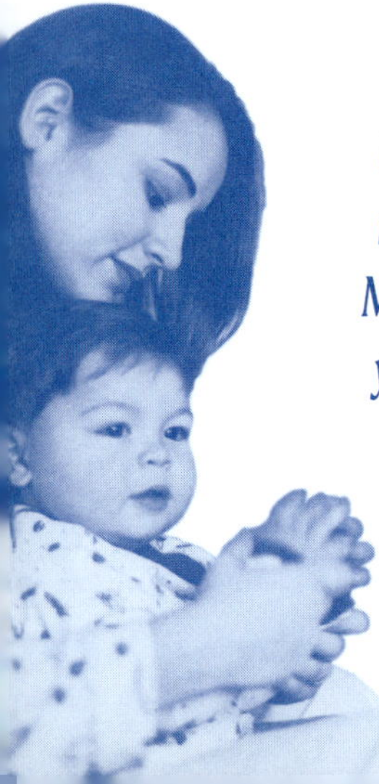

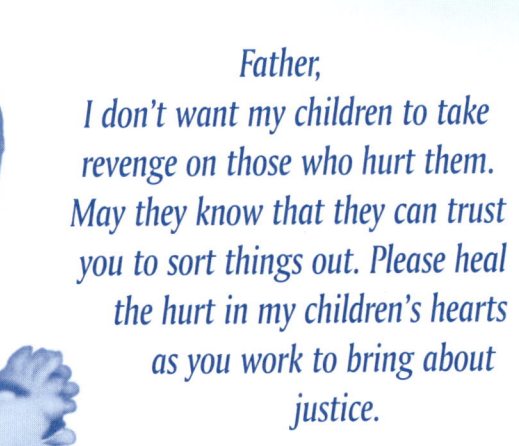

Psalm 1:1-3

'Blessed is the man who does not walk in the counsel of the wicked. . . .
But his delight is in the law of the Lord, . . .
He is like a tree planted by streams of water, . . .
Whatever he does prospers.'

*Father,
help my children to choose companions
who appreciate you, to take pleasure
in the guidelines you have given
them for their lives, to be secure
in their relationship with you
and to prosper in every
part of their lives.*

Exodus 20:12
'Honour your father and your mother,
so that you may live long in the land
the Lord your God is giving you.'

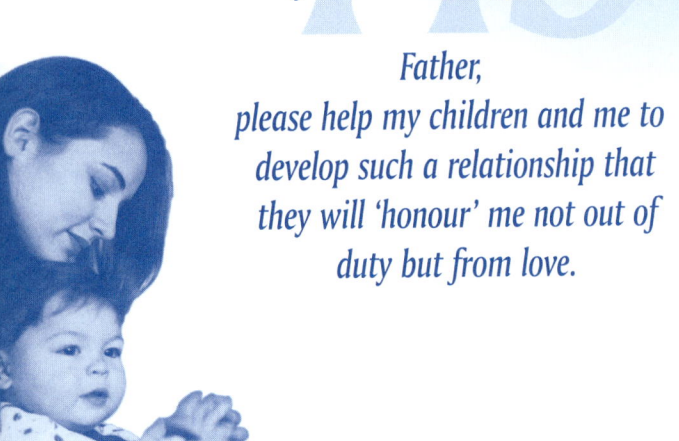

*Father,
please help my children and me to
develop such a relationship that
they will 'honour' me not out of
duty but from love.*

116

Proverbs 14:12
'There is a way that seems right to a man,
but in the end it leads to death.'

*Father,
I want my children to live for ever in
your kingdom. Show them clearly
that what may seem real to them
here is only a pretence; what is real,
is your world to come. Help them
to be ready for that.*

Ecclesiastes 3:1
'There is a time for everything,
and a season for every activity
under heaven.'

*Father,
I ask that my children will never be
part of the rat race, but will live
their lives with balance. As they
grow, help them always to take
time to work, have fun, rest
and sit with you.*

118

Titus 2:11-13
'For the grace of God
that brings salvation has appeared to all men.
It teaches us to say "No" to ungodliness
and worldly passions, and to live self-controlled,
upright and godly lives in this present age,
while we wait for the blessed hope.'

*Father,
thank you that your gift of
salvation is available to my
children. Help them to say 'Yes' to
it and to reflect you to those
around them.*

Psalm 25:21
'May integrity and uprightness protect me,
because my hope is in you.'

*Father of Integrity and Uprightness,
may goodness, honesty, honour,
purity, righteousness, virtue and
truth be a shield of protection
around my children.*

Romans 13:7
'Give everyone what you owe him.'

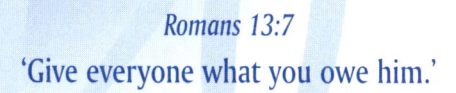

Father of Riches,
bless my children with the ability
to manage their finances well.
Help them not to fall into debt
with anyone.

Mark 1:35

'Very early in the morning, while it was still dark,
Jesus got up, left the house and went off
to a solitary place, where he prayed.'

*Father,
may my child be like your Child –
seeking your presence in the quiet
times of each day.*

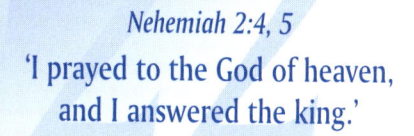

Nehemiah 2:4, 5
'I prayed to the God of heaven,
and I answered the king.'

*Father,
whenever my children need an
answer, let them ask for your
guidance first.*

Psalm 122:1
'I rejoiced with those who said to me,
"Let us go to the house of the Lord." '

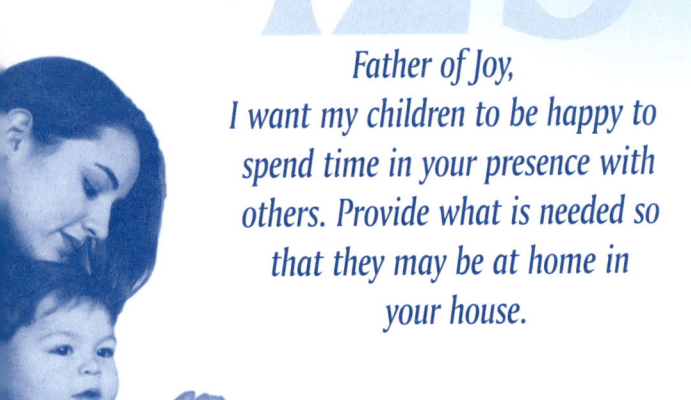

*Father of Joy,
I want my children to be happy to
spend time in your presence with
others. Provide what is needed so
that they may be at home in
your house.*

Psalm 127:2
'In vain you rise early and stay up late,
toiling for food to eat –
for he grants sleep to those he loves.'

*Father,
guard my children against becoming
'workaholics'. May they realise that
they do not work alone in providing
for their needs, for you are willing
to share that task with them.*

Matthew 28:20
'And surely I am with you always.'

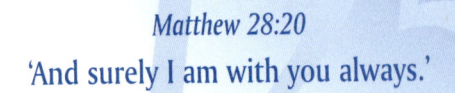

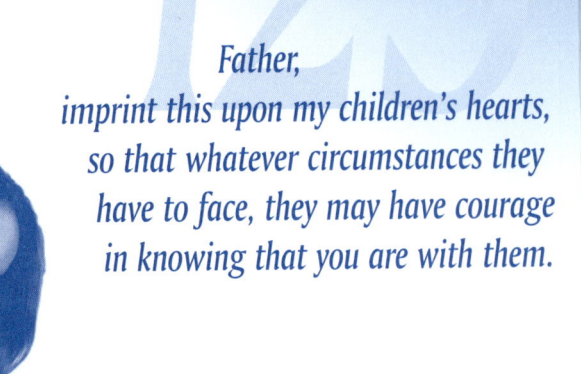

*Father,
imprint this upon my children's hearts,
so that whatever circumstances they
have to face, they may have courage
in knowing that you are with them.*